Tan Rosie®

Simply Vegan

Caribbean
Cookbook

by Karie-Ann Lee Sylvester & Monica Cudjoe

Tan Rosie Simply Vegan Caribbean Cookbook. Published in 2023 by Tan Rosie Foods Ltd.

Tan Rosie Foods Ltd
Unit 4 Chancel Way Industrial Estate, Chancel Way, Witton, Birmingham B6 7AU, England, United Kingdom.

© Copyright 2023 text, photography, and design: Karie-Ann Lee Sylvester & Monica Cudjoe, Tan Rosie Foods Ltd

www.tanrosie.com
Tan Rosie email: info@tanrosie.com
ISBN: 978-0-9572771-6-8

Social Media:
Twitter: @tanrosie
Facebook: Tan Rosie
Instagram: @tanrosiefoods
YouTube: Tan Rosie

Text © Copyright: Karie-Ann Lee Sylvester & Monica Cudjoe
Photographer © Copyright: Karie-Ann Lee Sylvester
Designer © Copyright: Karie-Ann Lee Sylvester
Front & Back Cover Photography: Paul Ward

Contents

Copyright 2

Dedication 5

Contents 3

Introduction 5

Tan Rosie Products 8

Veggie Info 9

Bakes 25

Rice Dishes 37

Soups & Stews 47

Dips & Things 57

Side Dishes 69

Mains 85

Desserts 113

Glossary 123

Index 127

This is for

Tanty Iris
grandmother, mother, aunt, cousin, and sister

Tan Rosie
grandmother, mother, and great grandmother

May they rest in eternal peace

introduction

Thank you for buying our latest book! Although we are not a vegan brand, most of the products we manufacture for Tan Rosie are suitable for vegans and over the years we have developed a strong and faithful vegan following. Mom and I are often asked about vegan recipe suggestions for this growing food movement that's happening globally right now, so I thought it was high time that I put pen to paper and create some vegan recipe ideas using Caribbean ingredients everyone will enjoy.

Throughout this book I wanted to show how you can use Caribbean ingredients to create interesting and tasty dishes in a very simple way. All of the Caribbean ingredients I've used in this book are very easy to find in large supermarkets, Asian, African stores or either online, so there's no excuse not to have a go and experiment.
I've focussed on a core selection of Caribbean ingredients my family have used in the UK especially, to create many of the dishes in this book. Plantains, green bananas, pumpkins, sweet potatoes, okras, coconuts, polenta and many more.

The recipes I've put together in this book will help you understand how to use ingredients you may have overlooked or have been reluctant to use before because of not knowing how to cook them. Once you get familiar with them, I have no doubt that you'll be using them more often in your cooking going forward.

This shift towards veganism or being plant based, is definitely not a trend with many more people incorporating more vegetables into their diets. This is why I think it's so important to try cooking with new ingredients to bring variety to your meals. It's so easy to keep buying the same veggies every time you go shopping, so I'm hoping this book will kick start your journey into experimenting with Caribbean vegetables forever!

The veggie info section at the start of this book is a great guide to the Caribbean ingredients we've used in the recipes throughout. Look at the different types of sweet potato are out there, varieties of plantains and their uses, key seasoning ingredients we use as a base for certain dishes, tips on the preparation of vegetables and much more.

I've also used some of the products we manufacture within some of the recipes in this book like our Aubergine & Mushroom Pesto, plantain crisps and Caribbean Style Curry Powder. Feel free to use whatever you have at hand to suit your needs (but they do taste rather good!).

Whether you are plant based, pescatarian, vegetarian, flexitarian or vegan, I hope by the end of this book you'll become much more confident in using readily available Caribbean ingredients to expand your plant based repertoire.

Karie-Ann Lee Sylvester

Tan Rosie products used in this book
available to buy at www.tanrosie.com

Veggie Info

Pulses & Grains

We use a variety of different pulses and grains in Caribbean cookery, and these are readily available in all supermarkets.

Dried: Simply soak overnight in cold water in the fridge, rinse out and bring to the boil, lower heat, and simmer for 45 minutes to 1 hour until soft, then incorporate into your dishes.
Tinned: These are ready to eat and time saving. Just drain and cook.

Kidney Beans: These are very commonly used in rice and peas dishes. Our it's eaten in stews or soups.

Chickpeas: These have been traditionally used in curries and dishes like Trinidad 'Doubles,' which is a fried dough with curried chickpeas.

Pigeon/Gungo Peas: Grenada for example where our family are from, would use pigeon/gungo peas in rice and peas, stews, soups. It can be made into many dishes. There's actually a pigeon pea festival in Trinidad where you can buy pigeon pea ice cream!

Black Eye Peas: Great for soups, stews etc.

Black Beans: Very popular in Cuba. They make their 'Rice and Peas' using this bean. Add to stews, soups and more.

Split Peas: Again, great in soups, stews, curries, and rice dishes.

Rice: Rice and peas traditionally uses long grain rice which tends to hold its' shape better and will continually absorb excess liquid after cooking.

Red/Green Lentils: Fantastic protein source and great in many dishes

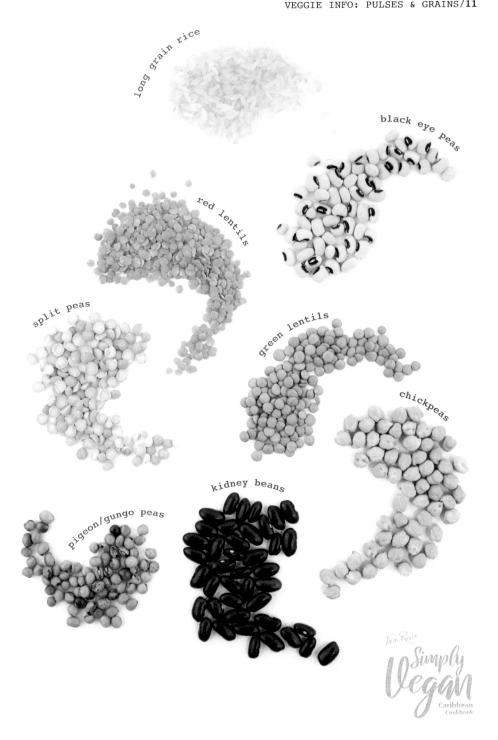

long grain rice

black eye peas

red lentils

split peas

green lentils

chickpeas

kidney beans

pigeon/gungo peas

Tan'Rosie
Simply
Vegan
Caribbean
Cookbook

Greens

We cook with an array of green vegetables in the Caribbean and some of which are easily available.

Callaloo: Tinned or fresh. Callaloo can be grown here if you want it fresh. My late father had an allotment, and this was one of the greens he grew in abundance! Spinach is very similar to Callaloo which is a great alternative. Callaloo is often available to buy in tins from supermarkets or more increasingly online.

Okra: Fresh or frozen. Also known as 'Ladies Fingers.' It's a delicious green vegetable we use in our cooking. The best way to get rid of the slime is to add lemon or lime.

Christophene: Fresh: Looks like a light green pear, with similar crisp flesh. Just wash, chop, cook like any other green vegetable and they're great in salads. It's a little harder to find depending on where you live, but it's worth hunting for them.

okra

callaloo

christophene

Tan'Rosie
Simply
Vegan
Caribbean
Cookbook

Roots

There are so many Caribbean root vegetables available in mainstream shops, you'll be spoilt for choice. Don't be intimidated by them! The general way to cook them is to treat them like a potato.

Orange Sweet Potato: Widely available and great for all sorts of dishes.

White Sweet Potato: Available in more speciality ethnic shops. Also known as 'Jamaican sweet potato.' It's flesh is firmer than the orange variety. We prefer using this type as there is much more flavour. It has a firm structure, so it's great for chips or in soups and stews. It has a deep red/purple skin with white flesh. It's usually more expensive than the orange variety, but worth testing out.

Yam: Available in speciality ethnic shops brown skin and white/yellow fresh. Firm structure and starchy. Great in soups, stews, chips and crisps.

Cassava: Available in most mainstream supermarkets and speciality shops. Brown skin and white flesh. Make sure you remove the centre stringy/fibrous centre before cooking. Treat like a potato. Great as chips and crisps. It's also made into flour which can be bought from speciality stores and online.

Eddoe/Coco: Also available at some mainstream supermarkets and speciality shops. Treat like a potato. Great in soups. Brown furry skin and white flesh.

oranage sweet potato

yam

eddoe/coco

cassava

white sweet potato

To n Rosie
Simply
Vegan
Caribbean
Cookbook

Plantain & Green Banana

Plantain is becoming increasingly popular here in the UK and it's really easy to find too. It's not a banana! It's in the banana family but you have to treat it like a potato, they must be cooked. It can be cooked in the skin, peeled and cooked in a variety of ways.

Green plantain: Usually larger and more angular than green bananas. They are unripe, so are not sweet. They have a firm texture and are great as crisps, chips, in soups or stews and much more.

Yellow (ripe) Plantain: These are ripe plantain which have a slight sweetness to taste. They are delicious fried, mashed, steamed, in soups and stews.

Yellow/Black (ripe/overripe) Plantain: These are overripe plantain that may look inedible to the untrained eye, but they are at their sweetest when the skin is black (even completely black), so don't throw them away! At this stage they are really soft and perfect mashed, steamed or fried or cooked in desserts.

Green Banana: These are very young bananas, but again they must be cooked! Try them out.

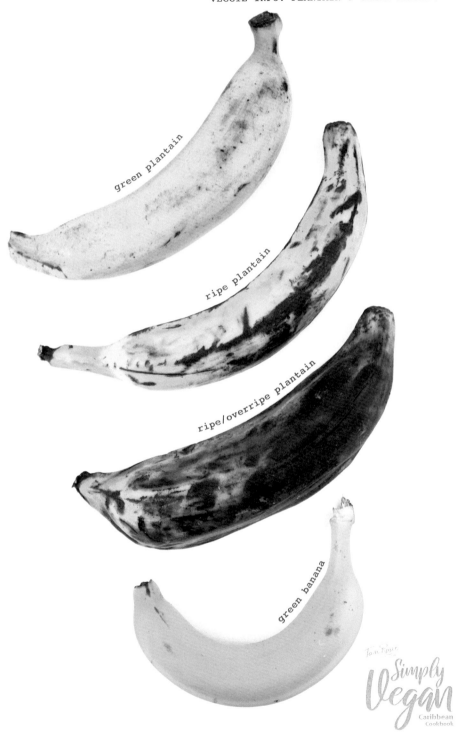

green plantain

ripe plantain

ripe/overripe plantain

green banana

Simply Vegan
Caribbean Cookbook

Other Fruit & Vegetables

Coconut: We use this delicious fruit in many savoury and sweet dishes. It's a stable ingredient in the Caribbean and great in a curry!

Breadfruit: This is one of our favourite veggies. When it's in season you can buy this in speciality African/Caribbean/Asian shops. It tastes like a potato, and you'd treat it in the same way, it's delicious. It's worth seeking out at these speciality stores to try it.

Pumpkin: Another staple Caribbean vegetable that is widely overlooked in the UK. Carving it out and using it just for Halloween is a travesty! There are many varieties to choose from when in season. We use it in dishes such as soups and stews, or we incorporate it into breads and desserts too. It's such a versatile ingredient that's super healthy. Alternatively, you can use **butternut squash** as it's more readily available in most supermarkets.

Corn: Corn has been grown traditionally across the Caribbean for generations which is eaten in its original form or it's often available dried, ground and made into polenta and cornmeal also known as 'Coo Coo' in Grenada and other islands. Due to the hot climate, drying corn has been essential technique used to preserve this ingredient. Coo Coo is a popular dish throughout many islands, and we've featured this ingredient in a selection of sweet and savoury dishes in the book.

Jackfruit: Jackfruit and breadfruit are from the same family. It's widely available in tins, but when it's in season you can also buy it fresh (which I highly recommend) from speciality African/Asian/Caribbean stores. It's a great meat substitute. The tinned variety tastes completely different to the fresh, so it's worth hunting down the fresh type to taste the difference.

Aubergine/Melongene/Egg Plant: This is a very popular ingredient in the Caribbean known by the above names depending on what island you are from. It's been grown in the Caribbean for many years and used in a variety of dishes.

Bell Peppers: Used in many dishes and widely available.

Lemon & Limes: Grown all over the Caribbean, they are used in both sweet and savoury dishes. Our family in Carriacou Grenada have tended to use limes more often in their dishes.

aubergine/melongene/egg plant

pumpkin

corn

coconut

bell peppers

lemon & lime

jackfruit

Simply Vegan
Caribbean Cookbook

Spices

Caribbean spices are staple ingredients and are available everywhere. Where possible, try to get the whole and freshly grind them to get the best flavour.

Allspice/Pimento: Available whole or ground. This is the key flavour in jerk seasoning. Add to savoury dishes like curries, seasonings and more. Ginger: A superb spice used widely in Caribbean cookery from sweet to savoury.

Cinnamon: A classic spice used equally in savoury and sweet dishes. There are different types of cinnamon available from ethnic speciality stores that vary in flavour such as the Chinese variety.

Nutmeg: Grenada's national spice pictured on their flag. It has a strong flavour used in cooking and for medicinal purposes. Visit the nutmeg factory in Grenada!

Paprika: We love this fragrant spice, also available smoked, hot. It really enriches savoury dishes.

Cloves: Another widely used spice used in different savoury dishes. Great used whole or ground.

Mace: This red spice surrounds the nutmeg seed and definitely packs a punch.

Turmeric: Great in curries and used to as a food colouring for our patties. It's a super spice!

Chillies (Scotch Bonnet/Red/Green Chillies): Not all Caribbean food is hot! We use chillies in very different ways to bring flavour to food, from using it whole in rice and curry dishes, to using a little of the skin in seasonings. Experiment to find out what works best for you.

chillies

allspice/pimento

ginger

turmeric

cloves

scotch bonnet pepper

nutmeg

cinnamon

paprika

Simply Vegan
Caribbean
Cookbook

Traditional Seasoning Combos

There is a common trend in the seasoning base for savoury dishes used in the Caribbean that you'll find in many recipes within this book. These core herbs, spices and vegetables help to create that authentic Caribbean flavour.

Many local shops in the Caribbean sell bundles of these select ingredients as they form the base for so many savoury dishes.

From our family experience in Carriacou Grenada, we have always used a pepper called 'seasoning pepper' which looks like a scotch bonnet, has tremendous flavour, but doesn't have the ferocious heat.

Thyme: It's a very important herb used in many savoury Caribbean dishes. It's grown on many islands. We prefer to use the fresh variety either chopped fine or add it whole on the stalk and remove after cooking.

Chilli (Scotch Bonnet/Red/Green Chillies): Not all Caribbean food is hot! We use chillies in very different ways to bring flavour to food, from using it whole in rice and curry dishes, to using a little of the skin in seasonings. Experiment to find out what works best for you.

Onion (Chive/White Onion/Spring Onion/Red Onion): Onions are another important base ingredient in Caribbean food. Traditionally chives and spring onion are used widely but use what's best available to you to bring that flavour to your dishes.

Celery: Chopped finely this delicious vegetable is used to enrich many dishes.

Garlic: Very important ingredient that we use a lot of. I use lots of garlic in this book, but please use the amount that works for you.

thyme

chillies

chives

celery

scotch bonnet pepper

spring onion

white onion

red onion

Simply Vegan
Caribbean Cookbook

Bakes

Pumpkin Flatbread

Pumpkin is a very popular vegetable eaten on many islands in Caribbean. It's such a tasty and healthy vegetables which can be used in a variety of ways. This is a quick and easy flat bread recipe for all to enjoy.

Makes 6

300g Self Raising Flour
½ tsp Baking Powder
800g Pumpkin (small/medium sized)

3 Tbsp Olive Oil for brushing
Nut milk to mix
Sea Salt
Black Pepper

Pumpkin Method:

1. Peel the pumpkin and chop into cubes. Line a baking tray with parchment paper, spread the pumpkin evenly on the tray, then drizzle with olive oil and a pinch of salt and black pepper.
2. Roast on a medium oven 200oC/gas mark 7 for 35 mins, or until cooked. (You can also peel, chop, and steam the pumpkin for speed).
3. In a bowl, mash the pumpkin with a fork or masher, cover and leave to cool.

Bread Method:

1. In a mixing bowl, add the flour, baking powder, 1 tsp salt, and 2 tbsp olive oil, rub together to form crumbs.
2. Add the mashed pumpkin and mix through.
3. Add almond milk a little at a time to form the dough.
4. Once the dough is formed, cover with cling film or a tea towel and leave to rest for 20 minutes.
5. Once the dough has rested, split the dough into 6 equal pieces.
6. Form each piece into a ball and put to one side.
7. On a floured surface, roll out each dough ball about 3mm thickness.
8. Place a frying pan on a medium/hot heat, then cook each flat bread for around 2 mins on each side or until golden brown. That's it!
9. Eat with curries, stews or as a sandwich. Enjoy.

Callaloo Roti

Callaloo is a green leafy vegetable and very similar to spinach and it's eaten widely across the Caribbean. You can easily buy it in tins online or from ethnic food shops.

Makes 6

2 Cups or 500g Strong Plain Flour
1 tsp Baking Flour
1 can Callaloo (540g tin)
½ tsp Black Pepper

¼ tsp Scotch Bonnet finely chopped
Olive Oil
Warm water to mix

Method:

1. In a sieve, drain the callaloo. Then place the callaloo in muslin or a tea towel and squeeze out the excess water, then place to one side.
2. In a mixing bowl, add the flour, baking powder, black pepper and 2 tbsp olive oil. Rub ingredients together to form crumbs.
3. Add the callaloo to the flour bowl and mix through.
4. Add warm water a little at a time to the bowl to form the dough.
5. Cover with a tea towel and leave to rest for 20 minutes.
6. Once the dough has rested, split the dough into 6 equal pieces.
7. Form each piece into a ball and put to one side.
8. On a floured surface, roll out each dough ball about 3mm thickness.
9. Place a frying pan on a medium/hot heat, add a little olive oil then fry each roti for around 2 mins on each side or until golden brown.

Tip: Spinach can be used as a substitute.

Plantain Bread

Plantain can be incorporated into many dishes just like a potato and this bread recipe compliments plantain well.

Makes 2 loaves

4 cups or 1kg Strong Bread Flour
500g Plantain, steamed and pureed and cooled
2 Tsp Yeast
100g Olive Oil
2 Tsp Salt

1 Tbsp Sugar
500ml Warmed nut milk

Method:

1. In a mixing bowl combine all the dry ingredients.
2. Add olive oil and blend in.
3. Combine all the ingredients with nut milk to form a soft dough.
4. Knead on a floured surface for 5 minutes.
5. Return to bowl and cover with a damp clean tea towel and rest for 1 hour.
6. After 1 hour knock back the dough and knead again.
7. Place dough into a bread tin lined with baking parchment or greased.
8. Cover and leave to rise for 45 minutes.
9. Preheat oven to gas mark 7.
10. Place dough in oven and bake for 35 to 40 minutes until golden brown.

Sweet Potato & Thyme Rolls

These sweet potato rolls use the most popular herb in Caribbean cuisine. They taste yummy as a dipping bread, sandwich, or quick snack.

Makes 10/12

Sweet Potato Ingredients:

400g Sweet Potato peeled, boiled, mashed
1 Medium White Onion finely chopped
1 Garlic Clove finely chopped
1 Bunch Fresh Thyme
finely chopped
1 Bunch Fresh Thyme
1 tsp Salt
1 tsp Black Pepper
Olive Oil for frying

Dough Ingredients:

2 Cups/500g Self Raising Flour
1 tsp Salt
1 tsp Baking Powder
2 Tbsp Olive Oil
1 tbsp Sugar
Warm water
400g Sweet potato mixture

Sweet Potato Method:

1. Place a frying pan on a medium heat. Add some olive oil and fry the onions until softened.
2. Add the garlic, salt, black pepper, 2 tbsp chopped thyme and mix through.
3. Add the mashed sweet potato and fry for 2 mins.
4. Remove from heat and leave to cool.

Dough Method:

1. In a mixing bowl, add the flour, baking powder, salt, and olive oil, rub together to form crumbs.
2. Add the sweet potato mixture and mix through.
3. Add warm water a little at a time to form the dough.
4. Once the dough is formed, cover with cling film or a tea towel and leave to rest for 20 minutes.
5. Once rested on a floured surface, roll out the dough ½ inch thick.
6. Using a pastry cutter, cut out each roll until all the dough has been used.
7. Place parchment paper in a baking tray or on a greased baking tray, and then place each roll evenly spaced out.
8. Brush each roll with olive oil and sprinkle with thyme.
9. Bake for 20 minutes at 200oC or gas mark

Plantain Stuffed Fried Dumplings

This is a lovely twist on fried dumplings using very ripe plantains. They make a great snack or yummy appetizer.

Serves 4/6

Plantain Ingredients:

2 Very ripe Plantains (black/yellow colour) peeled & diced into 1cm	1 tbsp Fresh Thyme	
	½ tsp Salt	
	1 tsp Black Pepper	
2 Spring onions	1 Red chilli	
1 Garlic Clove crushed or finely chopped	1 Green chilli	
	Olive Oil	
	Water to seal	

Dough Ingredients:

2 Cups/500g Self Raising Flour	vegetable oil for shallow frying
1 tsp Salt	
2 Tbsp Olive Oil	
1 tbsp Sugar	
Nut milk	

Plantain Method:

1. Place a frying pan on a medium heat. Add some olive oil and fry the onions until softened.
2. Add the diced plantain and fry for 2 mins.
3. Add the garlic, salt, black pepper, 2 tbsp chopped thyme and mix through.
4. Cook for a further 3 or 4 mins or until the plantain is cooked turns yellow.
5. Remove from heat and leave to cool.

Dough Method:

1. In a mixing bowl, add the flour, baking powder, salt, and olive oil, rub together to form crumbs.
2. Add the nut milk a little at a time to form the dough.
3. Once the dough is formed, cover with cling film or a tea towel and leave to rest for 20 minutes.
4. Once rested on a floured surface, roll out the dough 3mm thick.
5. Using a pastry cutter, cut out each circle of dough until all the dough has been used.
6. In the middle of the dough circle, add a tablespoon of plantain mixture.
7. Using your finger, dip into water and add water to half of the outer edge of the dough circle. Fold the dry edge over to meet the wet edge and press down to seal the dumpling.
8. With a fork, crimp the pressed edge to fully seal, then pierce the top of the dumpling (this lets out the hot air, so it doesn't burst when frying).
9. In a saucepan, add 1 inch of vegetable oil (around 170oC). To test the oil heat, add a tiny piece of dough to the hot oil, if it bubbles and rises to the top quickly, the oil is ready to use.
10. Cook each dumpling for around 2 minutes each side (basting as you go) until golden brown. Place on kitchen roll when cooked and serve with a dip (Tan Rosie Sweet Chilli Ginger Sauce pictured). Yum!

Rice Dishes

Spicy Rice Corn Fritters

This fritter recipe is a fun way to use up left over rice for a quick snack or appetizer. Virtually any ingredient can be used in the batter to add extra flavour. Eat with a spicy dip.

Makes 15

2 Cups cooked long grain rice, cooled
1 Tin Sweet Corn 600g
1 tbsp Fresh Thyme
1 Red Chilli
1 Green Chill

½ Red Bell pepper (small) diced
½ Green Bell pepper (small) diced
½ Yellow Bell pepper (small) diced
3 Spring onions

2 Garlic cloves
2 tsp Egg Replacement or Flax seeds
1 ½ tsp Salt
1 tsp Black Pepper
1 ½ cups Plain Flour
Nut milk for

mixing
Vegetable Oil for shallow frying

Method:

1. Place all ingredients except the last two into a mixing bowl and mix through.
2. Add the nut milk little by little to form a batter of 'dropping consistency' or 'sticky.'
3. Cover with cling film and leave to rest for 20 minutes.
4. In a saucepan, add 1 inch of vegetable oil (around 170oC). To test the oil heat, add a tiny piece of dough to the hot oil, if it bubbles and rises to the top quickly, the oil is ready to use.
5. Using a dessert spoon, scoop the batter into the hot oil being careful not to overcrowd the pan, and cook for a few minutes each side (keep basting each fritter with oil)
6. Once each fritter is golden brown remove from the pan to drain onto a plate lined with kitchen roll to cool.
7. Serve with a dipping sauce of your choice. Yum!

Red Pepper Spiced Rice

If you're looking for a rice dish that is flavourful, quick, and easy, then try this delicious red pepper dish. It features our Caribbean Sweet Pepper Sauce which is very mild in heat but has bags of flavour.

Serves 4/6

2 Cups Long grain rice
1 Large Red Bell Pepper diced
2 Jars Tan Rosie Caribbean Sweet Pepper Sauce
2 Garlic cloves

finely chopped
1 Medium white onion finely chopped
1 tbsp Fresh thyme
1 tsp Salt
1 tsp Black Pepper
600ml Vegeta-

ble/vegan stock
Olive Oil for frying
½ Scotch Bonnet Pepper (option-al)

Method:

1. Wash the rice in a bowl with 3 or 4 changes of cold water to remove excess starch, then put to one side.
2. In a frying pan on a medium heat, add 2 tbsp olive oil and fry the onions for a few minutes until softened.
3. Add the garlic, salt, black pepper, scotch bonnet pepper and thyme, then stir.
4. Add the red bell pepper and stir through.
5. Add the rice and stir.
6. Add the 2 jars of Caribbean Sweet Pepper Sauce and stir.
7. Add the vegetable stock, then bring to the boil, cover with a lid, turn down to a very low heat and cook for 20 mins.
8. After 20 mins, check the rice to see if it's cooked. If so, remove from heat, cover, and leave it to continue to absorb any liquid for 5/8 minutes.
9. With a fork, gently fluff up the rice, check the seasoning, adjust if needed and serve.

Curry Rice & Peas

Transform classic rice and peas into an even more tasty side dish or meal with this curry twist. You can also substitute pigeon peas with red kidney beans.

Serves 4/6

2 Cups Long grain rice
1 tin Pigeon Peas or red kidney beans
1 large White Onion finely chopped
2 Garlic cloves finely chopped

1 tbsp fresh thyme
1 scotch bonnet chilli (optional)
1 tsp Salt
1 tsp Black Pepper
1 tin Coconut Milk

300ml Vegetable/vegan stock
1 packet Tan Rosie Caribbean Style Curry Powder

Method:

1. Wash the rice in a bowl with 3 or 4 changes of cold water to remove excess starch, then put to one side.
2. In a frying pan on a medium heat, add the onions and fry for 3 or 4 minutes or until softened.
3. Add the garlic, thyme, salt, black pepper, curry powder and stir.
4. Add the rice, drained gungo peas and stir.
5. Add the coconut milk, vegetable stock and stir.
6. Add the whole scotch bonnet pepper (keeping it intact with the stalk) and bring to the boil.
7. Turn the heat down very low, cover and cook for 20 mins.
8. After 20 mins, check the rice to see if it's cooked. If so, remove from heat, cover, and leave it to continue to absorb any liquid for 5/8 minutes.
9. With a fork, gently fluff up the rice, check the seasoning, adjust if needed and serve. Don't forget to remove the scotch bonnet pepper!

Okra Fried Rice

Okra is a delicious green vegetable which can be eaten raw or cooked. It tastes amazing in this fried rice dish which can be eaten as a main meal or a side dish and it's not slimy!

Serves 2/3

1 Cup cooked long grain rice (washed)
10 Okra fingers, trimmed, and sliced
1 Medium white onion
2 Garlic cloves finely chopped
1 Green chilli finely chopped
½ Red Bell Pepper chopped
½ Green Bell Pepper chopped
½ Yellow Bell Pepper chopped
1 tsp Salt
1 tsp Black Pepper
1 tbsp Fresh Thyme
1 tsp veg stock or ½ stock cube crumbled
Olive oil for frying

Method:

1. In a saucepan, par boil the rice for 10 minutes then drain. Put to one side.
2. In a frying pan on a medium heat, add some olive oil and fry off the onions for a few minutes until softened.
3. Add the red, green, and yellow bell peppers and cook for 1 minute.
4. Add the garlic, thyme, green chilli, salt, black pepper and stir.
5. Add the chopped okra and mix through.
6. Add the rice and veg stock and cook for a further 1 minute.
7. Adjust the seasoning, if necessary, then lower heat, cover and leave for 5 minutes until the rice is cooked through and serve.

Tip: Use lemon or lime juice to cut down on the sliminess of the okra.

Soups & Stews

Black Bean & Coconut Stew

Black beans are very popular in Cuba and is normally cooked with rice,
but it's just as tasty cooked in coconut milk to form a hearty stew.
Give it a try.

Serves 2/3

*2 tins Black
Beans, drained
1 Tin Coconut
milk
300ml Vegeta-
ble/vegan stock
1 Medium white
onion
2 Garlic cloves
finely chopped*

*1 Scotch bonnet
chilli (whole)
optional
1 tsp Salt
1 tsp Black
Pepper
1 tbsp Fresh
Thyme
Olive oil for
frying*

Method:

1. Place a saucepan on a medium heat, add 2 tbsp olive oil and sauté
    the onions for 3 or 4 mins until they are soft.
2. Add the garlic, thyme, salt, black pepper and stir.
3. Add the coconut milk and vegetable stock and stir.
4. Add the black beans and whole scotch bonnet, bring to the boil
    whilst continually stirring ensuring it doesn't stick.
5. Cook the liquid down on a medium to high heat until the liquid has
    thickened and reduce.
6. Remove from the heat and serve with white rice and steamed vegeta-
    bles. Don't forget to remove the scotch bonnet!

Pigeon Pea & Corn Dumpling Soup

Pigeon peas, also known as gungo peas, are grown all over the Caribbean. They are used in soups, stews, and rice dishes. They're super tasty, a great source of protein and taste delicious in this soup with the corn dumplings.

Serves 4

Dumpling Ingredients:

1 Cup/250g Fine Cornmeal
1 Cup/250g Plain Flour
1 tsp Salt
2 tbsp Olive oil for frying
Warm water to mix

2 tins Pigeon Peas
3 Carrots, peeled & finely diced
1 Large potato peeled & finely diced
3 Celery sticks, diced

Soup Ingredients:

3 Garlic cloves finely chopped
1 tsp Salt
1 tsp Black pepper
1 Scotch bonnet chilli (optional)
1 tin Coconut milk

1 Litre vegetable/vegan stock
2 tbsp Olive oil

Dumpling Method 1:

1. In a mixing bowl, add the cornmeal, self-raising flour, olive oil and salt, then mix into crumbs.
2. Add warm water a little at a time to the flour to create a firm dough.
3. Cover with a tea towel or cling film and rest for 20 mins.

Soup Method:

1. Place a large saucepan on a medium heat, add the olive oil, then add the onions and fry for 2 minutes until softened.
2. Add the carrots and stir for 1 minute.
3. Add the celery and stir though.
4. Add the salt, black pepper, and pigeon peas, then stir.
5. Add the coconut milk and vegetable stock, then bring to the boil.
6. Cover, lower the heat and simmer for 5 minutes.
7. Using a stick blender, blend the soup into fine consistency and return to a low heat then cover.

Dumpling Method 2:

1. On a floured surface, knead the dough for a minute, then create 10/12 round dumplings (you can be creative with the shape).
2. Once you have formed all your dumplings, place them in the soup and cook for around 20 mins or until the dumplings are cooked and serve.

Tip: Dry peas can be used. Simply soak overnight in cold water then cook for 40 minutes in fresh water.

Curried Sweet Potato & Cashew Nut Soup

This is a very rustic, hearty soup with using an orange sweet potato. We often use the white sweet potato as it's less watery than the orange variety. You buy the white variety in any ethnic grocery store. The cashew nuts give a delicious crunch to the soup.

Serves 3/4

400g Sweet Potato
2 Garlic cloves, finely chopped
1 large red onion finely chopped
3 Carrots peeled and diced
Olive oil for frying
1 tsp Allspice
2 tbsp Fresh Thyme
½ Red chilli pepper
1 litre vegetable/vegan stock
3 Celery sticks chopped
1 Packet Tan Rosie Caribbean Style Curry Powder
130g Cashew nuts
1 tsp Salt
1 tsp Black Pepper

Method:

1. Place a large saucepan on a medium heat, add 2 tbsp olive oil and fry off the red onions for 1 minute.
2. Add the diced carrots and stir for 1 minute.
3. Add the celery and sweet potato and cook for a further 2 minutes.
4. Add the thyme, chilli, salt, 3 quarters of the cashew nuts, black pepper, allspice, and curry powder and stir through.
5. Add the vegetable stock and bring to the boil.
6. Reduce the heat, cover, and simmer for 15-20 minutes until the sweet potato is cooked.
7. At this stage, you can either serve it in this chunky rustic texture or you can use a stick blender to get a smooth consistency.
8. Spoon into a bowl then sprinkle the remaining cashew nuts on top and serve.

Green Lentil & Plantain Stew

Green lentil and very ripe plantain work well together in this chunky stew. Ensure you buy ripe plantain (the blacker the skin, the better) for this dish as they'll be super soft and extra sweet.

Serves 2/3

3 Overripe Plantain 5mm sliced
1 tin green lentils drained
2 Garlic cloves finely chopped
1 medium white onion finely chopped

1 tbsp Fresh Thyme
½ tsp Salt
½ tsp Black Pepper
½ tsp Allspice
300ml Vegetable/Vegan stock
Olive oil for frying

½ green chilli finely chopped

Method:

1. Place a saucepan on a medium heat, add 2 tbsp olive oil and add the onions. Fry until softened.
2. Add the garlic, thyme, green chilli and plantain and fry for 1 minute.
3. Add the green lentils and stir and cook for 3 or minutes.
4. Add the salt, black pepper, and vegetable stock, stir, cover, and reduce the heat and simmer for 5-8 minutes.
5. Remove from the heat and serve with steamed vegetables.

Pigeon Pea Bush taken in Grenada

Dips & Things

Jerk Paste

This jerk paste recipe is simple to make and has bags of flavour. You can make it in advance and freeze it for future use. Adjust the amount of chilli pepper to your own taste and you can use this on multiple dishes to add extra flavour.

Makes 1 batch

4 Spring Onions
½ Lime
2 tsp Allspice
2 tbsp Fresh Root Ginger
2 tbsp Fresh Thyme
½ Scotch Bonnet Pepper
1 tsp Freshly Ground Nutmeg
½ tsp Fresh Ground Cloves
1 tsp Black Pepper
1 tsp Salt
100ml Olive Oil to form paste

Method:

1. Place all ingredients in a food processor and blend until it's a smooth paste. You can also use a stick blender to form the paste.

Tips:

1. You can also use a pestle and mortar to form the paste.
2. To make more of a sauce add orange juice, Worcestershire sauce, soya sauce and rum (optional).
3. You can decant into small tubs and freeze for future use.
4. Keeps well in the fridge for up to 3 days.

Black Eye Pea Dip

Black eye peas are a great source of protein and can be used in many ways. It's another popular Caribbean pulse and tastes great as a dip. It's amazing spread onto crusty bread or with crisps as a delicious snack. You can also use dried black eye peas which you can rehydrate and cook before making this dip instead of tinned varieties. Try it!

Serves 2/3

*1 Tin Black Eye
Peas, drained
1 Medium white
Onion finely
chopped
3 Cloves
Garlic, crushed
1/2 Red Chilli
finely chopped
2 tbsp Fresh*

*Parsley finely
chopped
Olive Oil
½ tsp Salt
½ Black Pepper*

Method:

1. Place a saucepan on a medium heat with 2 tbs olive oil, add the onions and fry for a few minutes until softened.
2. Add the garlic, thyme, parsley, salt, and black pepper and stir.
3. Add the black eye peas and cook for a few minutes.
4. Remove from the heat then add 4/5 tbsp of olive oil.
5. Mash or blend with a stick blender, potato masher or fork until it's a smooth consistency and serve.

Tip: To use dried peas, simply soak the peas in cold water overnight, then boil for around 40 minutes.

Roasted Corn & Red Pepper Dip

Corn is such an important vegetable in the Caribbean. Our family have often roasted it, make it into Coo Coo also known as polenta, dumplings and more. You can eat this dip on toast, in a sandwich or mixed through rice or cous cous.

Serves 2/3

2 Red Bell Peppers, halved and deseeded
2 Corn on the cobs
1 tsp Vegetable stock
Salt
Black Pepper
¼ Chilli Pepper

finely chopped
1 tbsp Fresh Thyme finely chopped
Olive Oil

Method:

1. Line a baking tray with parchment paper and place the bell peppers and corn. Drizzle with olive oil and add ½ tsp of salt and ½ tsp black pepper, then roast in the oven for 20 mins on 200oC or gas mark 7/8.
2. With a sharp knife cut the corn off the cobs.
3. In a mixing bowl place the roasted corn, bell peppers, vegetable stock, ½ tsp salt, ½ tsp black pepper, chilli pepper, thyme and 3 tbsp olive oil.
4. Combine all ingredients together using a stick blender or food processor and serve.

Tip: Try not to blend the dip too smoothly as it tastes better with some bite!

Roasted Pumpkin & Coconut Spread

Try this simple pumpkin spread with chips or crackers as an appetizer or snack. You can substitute pumpkin with butternut squash too.

Serves 2/3

700g Pumpkin peeled & diced
100ml Coconut Milk
Salt
½ White onion finely chopped
1 Garlic clove finely chopped
1 tsp Fresh thyme finely chopped
Black Pepper
½ Chilli Pepper (optional)
1 tsp Vegetable Stock
Pumpkin seeds

Method:

1. Place some parchment paper in a baking tray, pop in the peeled, diced pumpkin. Drizzle with olive oil and sprinkle with, onion, garlic, thyme, ½ tsp salt and ½ black pepper.
2. Roast in a medium oven, 200oC/gas mark 7/8, for 40/45 mins, or until nicely roasted.
3. In a mixing bowl, place the roasted pumpkin, coconut milk, 1 tsp salt, 1 tsp black pepper, 1 tsp vegetable stock and blend/mash with a stick blender or place in a food processer.
4. Blend until smooth and serve with a sprinkling of pumpkin seeds.

Tip: This dip can be portioned out and frozen for future use.

Pigeon Pea & Garlic Spread

This is another way to experiment with one the most popular pulses in the Caribbean and in our home. It's very quick to make and you can also add chilli to recipe to give it a good kick!

Serves 2/3

2 Tins Pigeon
Pes (Gungo
Peas), drained
4 Garlic Cloves
½ White onion
finely chopped
½ tsp Salt
½ tsp Black
Pepper
Olive Oil

Method:

1. Place a saucepan on a medium heat, add 2 tbsp olive oil and fry the onions for 3 minutes until softened.
2. Add the garlic and fry for a few seconds.
3. Add the pigeon peas, salt, black pepper, stir through and cook for 3 minutes.
4. Take the pan off the heat and add 4/5 tbsp olive oil. Mash all ingredients together using a masher, stick blender or potato masher, into a smooth consistency, and serve.

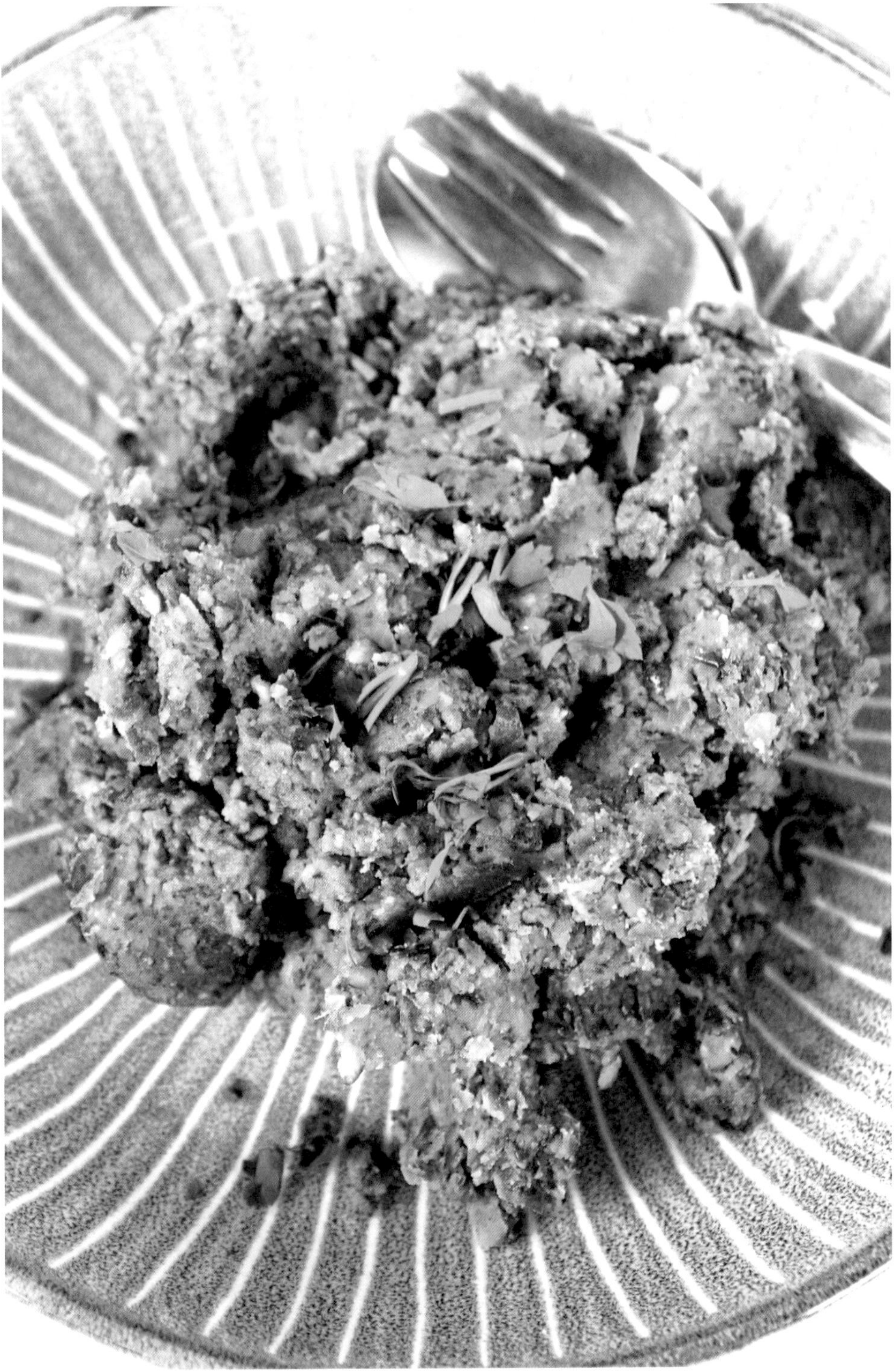

Side Dishes

Jerk Roasted Pumpkin

The jerk paste in the dips section of this book is the perfect seasoning for any vegetable. We've chosen some pumpkin to show you how you can use the paste in a quick and easy way. It's delicious!

Serves 2/3

700g Pumpkin
peeled & diced
4 tbsp Olive
Oil
4 tbsp Jerk
Paste (Dips &
Things chapter)

Method:

1. In a bowl place the diced pumpkin, jerk paste, and olive oil then massage. Ensure the pumpkin is well coated with the jerk paste seasoning.
2. Turn the seasoned pumpkin out onto a baking tray lined with parchment paper.
3. Roast in an oven at 200oC/gas mark 7/8 for 30/40 mins or until cooked through.

Curry Chickpea Fritters

As a family we love fritters. You can make fritters out of pretty much any vegetable to create a tasty snack. We've used our curry powder with chickpea flour to elevate the traditional fritter. Serve with a spicy dip of your choice.

Makes 15/20

1 Tin Chick-
peas, drained
4 Spring
Onions, chopped
¼ Scotch Bonnet
Pepper
1 tsp Salt
1 tsp Black
Pepper
1 tsp Baking

Powder
1 cup/250g
Chickpea Flour
1 tsp Egg
replacement or
flax seeds
Coconut Milk
2 tsp Tan Rosie
Caribbean Style
Curry Powder

Sunflower Oil
    for frying

Method:

1. In a mixing bowl place the chickpea flour, salt, black pepper, scotch bonnet, curry powder, spring onions, baking powder, egg replacement and mix through.
2. Add the coconut little by little to create a batter. This needs to be dropping consistency or sticky. If it gets too runny, add more chickpea flour and allow to rest for around 20 minutes covered with cling film.
3. In a saucepan, heat 1 inch of sunflower oil to a medium to hot heat (around 170oC). Once you think the oil is hot enough, test with a small amount of the batter. If it sizzles and rises to top very quickly, then the oil is ready.
4. Using a tablespoon, drop spoonful's of the batter into the hot oil, try not to overcrowd the pan. Baste each spoonful whilst it's cooking in the pan. Cook each fritter for 2/3 mins on each side whilst continuously basting.
5. Once each fritter has turned golden brown remove and place to drain on a plate with kitchen roll.
6. Serve with a tasty dip.

'Hard Food' Salad

Potato salad doesn't have to be made from Maris Piper's or King Edward's! Experiment with Caribbean root vegetables to create an extra special salad.

Serves 3/4

1 Small White or Orange Sweet Potato, peeled & diced
500g Cassava, peeled & diced
1 Small Taro, peeled and diced
Vegan Mayonnaise
3 Spring Onions, finely chopped
Salt
1 tbsp Flat leaf parsley finely chopped
½ tsp Black Pepper
1 tbsp Tan Rosie's Garlic & Pepper Sauce (optional)

Method:

1. Fill a saucepan the hot water and boil the chopped sweet potato, cassava, and taro with ½ tsp salt until cooked.
2. Drain and transfer to a mixing bowl.
3. Add 3 tbsp of mayonnaise, ½ tsp salt, black pepper, hot sauce, spring onions, parsley and mix and serve.

Green Plantain Rosti

You can treat plantains like potatoes and this is another great recipe twist to incorporate this tropical ingredient in a popular dish. Make sure the plantain is green/unripe and firm.

Makes 15

2 Green Plan-
tain, peeled &
grated
1 tsp Egg
replacement
1 tbs Plain
Flour
½ tsp Baking
Powder
2 Spring Onion

1 tbsp Thyme
½ tsp Salt
Sunflower Oil
for frying

Method:

1. In a mixing bowl place all ingredients except the sunflower oil and mix.
2. In a saucepan, heat 1 inch of sunflower oil to a medium to hot heat (around 170oC). Once you think the oil is hot enough, test with a small amount of the batter. If it sizzles and rises to top very quickly, then the oil is ready.
3. Using a tablespoon, drop spoonsful of the batter into the hot oil, try not to overcrowd the pan. Baste each spoonful whilst it's cooking in the pan. Cook each fritter for 2/3 mins on each side whilst continuously basting.
4. Once each rosti has turned golden brown remove and place to drain on a plate with kitchen roll.
5. Serve with a tasty dip (Tan Rosie Sweet Chilli Ginger Dip pictured).

Bajan Style Cou Cou & Okra

Cou Cou is also known as polenta. It's made from dried corn which is ground into a coarse or fine powder. It's used heavily across many Caribbean islands and can be combined with different pulses or vegetables like okra as a side dish or part of a main meal. Our Grenadian heritage makes 'coo coo' and okra separately compared to this Barbadian dish combining the two components together.

Serves 4

10/15 Okra fingers, trimmed and chopped
1 cup/250g Polenta
400mls Coconut Milk
200ml Vegetable Stock

1 Medium Onion, finely chopped
2 Garlic cloves, finely chopped
2 tbsp Fresh Thyme finely chopped
Olive Oil
¼ Scotch Bonnet

pepper, deseeded finely chopped (optional)

Method:

1. Place a saucepan on a medium heat, add 2 tbsp olive oil, onions, and sauté for 5 minutes until translucent.
2. Add the garlic, stir, and cook for a further 1 minute.
3. Add the thyme, coconut milk, vegetable stock, salt, black pepper, and scotch bonnet and bring to the boil.
4. Reduce heat and simmer for 15 minutes.
5. Add the chopped okra and stir through.
6. Add polenta, stirring continuously to avoid forming any lumps. Extra water can be added if necessary to create a loose consistency.
7. Cook for 5 minutes. If using cornmeal, the cooking time will be much longer at around 30 minutes.

Tip: Using cornmeal will take longer to cook than polenta. Polenta is precooked and dried to takes a shorted time to cook.

Lime Chilli Whole Baked Plantain

Plantain is such a versatile ingredient and the simplest way to cook it is to bake it whole. The lime and chilli enhance the flavour of the plantain. It's best to use the ripest plantain you can find. The blacker the skin the better and sweeter!

Serves 2/3

*4 Very Ripe
Plantain
(black/yellow
colour) peeled
2 Limes, halved
1 Red Chilli,
finely sliced
1 Green Chilli
finely sliced
Olive Oil*

*½ tsp Salt
½ tsp Black
Pepper*

Method:

1. Line a baking tray with parchment paper.
2. Place the plantains on the tray, liberally drizzle with olive oil and sprinkle the chillies, salt, black pepper over the plantain.
3. Squeeze to halves of lime over the plantain and place them on the tray with the plantain.
4. Roast in a medium oven, 200oC/gas mark 7/8, for 35/40 minutes until cooked.

Baked Curry Cauliflower

Transform the humble cauliflower with this simple baked curry seasoning. Add some chopped nuts or sprinkle with seeds to add extra crunch to this fragrant dish.

Serves 2/3

1 large cauli-
flower
Olive Oil
1 pack Tan
Rosie Caribbean
Style Curry
Powder

Method:

1. Chop the cauliflower into chunks and place on a baking tray.
2. Drizzle the cauliflower with olive oil and rub in 2 tbsp curry powder, and massage through.
3. Put in the oven to roast for 25-30 minutes, 200oC/gas mark 7/8. Turn over cauliflower halfway then serve with coconut rice, fresh greens ad a chutney.

Eddoe/Coco

Mains

Pumpkin Macaroni Pie

Macaroni pie or mac 'n' cheese is a popular comfort food eaten across many Caribbean islands. This is a great twist on this traditional dish using pumpkin. You can also use butternut squash as an alternative. It's yum!

Serves 4

250g Macaroni	crushed.	200g Vegan
1 small Pump-	½ Red chilli	Cheese, grated.
kin/Butternut	deseeded finely	3 tbsp Plain
squash peeled	chopped	Four
and diced, and	Olive Oil	500ml Nut Milk
par boiled.	2 sprigs Fresh	Salt
1 medium onion	Thyme	Black Pepper
finely chopped.	300 Breadcrumbs	
2 garlic	1 tbsp Smoked	
cloves,	Paprika	

Pumpkin Method:

1. Place a saucepan on a medium heat, add 2 tbsp olive oil, onions, and sauté for 5 minutes until translucent.
2. Add the garlic, stir, and cook for a further 1 minute.
3. Add diced par boiled pumpkin and sauté until softened for 2 minutes.
4. Add thyme, ½ tsp salt and ½ tsp black pepper.
5. Remove from heat and transfer to a separate bowl.

Cheese Sauce Method:

1. In a saucepan, place 2 tbsp olive and the flour and cook for 1 minute. Add the nut milk, 1 tsp salt and 1 tsp black pepper, and bring to the boil.
2. Stir in the vegan cheese until melted and until sauce is thickened.
3. Remove from heat and cover.

Macaroni Method:

1. Boil the macaroni until cooked, drain and put to one side.
2. In an oven dish, place the cooked macaroni, pumpkin mixture, and coat with the cheese sauce. Mix through.
3. Place the breadcrumbs in a bowl with the smoked paprika and blend.
4. Sprinkle the breadcrumbs over the macaroni and bake in the oven at 220oC for 20 minutes.
5. Serve with fresh steamed greens.

Black Eye Pea & Sweet Potato Curry

Try this simple curry recipe which utilises tasty black eye peas. It's a hearty recipe and tastes great with sweet potato. Serve with plain rice or roti.

Serves 2/3

1 tin Black Eye Peas
600g Sweet potato, peeled and diced
1 medium onion finely diced
2 Garlic cloves, crushed
1 Scotch Bonnet Pepper
200ml Vegetable stock
1 packet Tan Rosie Caribbean Style Curry Powder
1 tin Coconut Milk
1 tsp Salt
1 tsp Black Pepper
2 Sprigs fresh thyme
Olive Oil

Method:

1. Place a frying pan on a medium heat, add 3 tbsp olive oil, diced onions and sauté for 3 mins or until softened.
2. Add the garlic, thyme, salt & black pepper and stir.
3. Add the sweet potato and stir.
4. Add 2 heaped tbsp of Tan Rosie Caribbean Curry Powder and stir.
5. Add the coconut milk and vegetable stock, scotch bonnet pepper (keep whole with stalk on), then bring to the boil.
6. Add the black eye peas and stir. Lower heat and simmer for 15 minutes or until the potato is cooked and sauce is thickened.
7. Serve with white rice, a fragrant chutney, and a salad.

Tip:

Make sure when you stir, don't burst the scotch bonnet pepper! Before serving, remember to remove it.

Jerk Tofu Skewers

Jerk seasoning works exceptionally well on tofu, adding tremendous flavour to this tasty protein. These skewers are great in the oven on pop them on the barbeque for extra flavour.

Serves 4

1 pack of firm
tofu
3 tbsp jerk
paste (Dips &
Things chapter)
1 large red
onion
Olive Oil
Wooden skewers

Method:

1. Pat dry or squeeze out any excess liquid from the tofu.
2. Chop the tofu and red onion into 1-inch chunks.
3. In a bowl add the jerk paste with 4 tbsp olive oil and mix into a lose consistency.
4. Form your skewers with the red onion and tofu, alternating chunks.
5. Baste the jerk seasoning onto the skewers, then bake in the oven for 20 minutes (turn halfway), on 220oC or gas mark 7/8.
6. Serve with rice, salad, and a spicy dip. Yum! (Tan Rosie Sweet Chilli Ginger Dip pictured).

Tips:
1. You can remove excess liquid from tofu using a tofu press!
2. These skewers can also be cooked on the barbeque.

Caribbean Wellington

Wellington's are not just for beef! We've fused some easy to find Caribbean ingredients to form this delicious wellington which also uses our Aubergine & Mushroom Pesto as a duxelles.

Serves 4

200g Sweet Potato, peeled, small diced.
200g Green lentils (tinned)
1 tbsp Jerk Paste (Dips & Things chapter) or Tan Rosie's Jerk Rub
100g Pecan nuts

rough chopped.
2 Garlic cloves finely chopped.
1 ½ sticks Celery finely chopped.
1 Onion finely chopped.
1 Carrot peeled and diced.
1 tbsp Vegetable stock

100g Bread-crumbs
1 Red chilli, deseeded and finely chopped.
½ tsp Salt
½ tsp Black Pepper
1 Jar Tan Rosie Aubergine & Mushroom Pesto & Spread for

the duxelles.
Vegan Pastry premade
Olive Oil
1 tbsp Fresh Thyme finely chopped.
1 tbsp Flax Seeds in water to form paste or egg replacement.

Filling Method:

1. Place a saucepan on a medium heat and add 3 tbsp olive. Fry the onions for 3 minutes until softened.
2. Add the sweet potato and cook for 3/4 minutes.
3. Add the carrots and celery and cooked for 2 minutes.
4. Add the garlic, chilli, thyme, salt, black pepper and cook for 2 minutes or until the sweet potato is cooked.
5. Add the green lentils, vegetable stock and stir.
6. Cover, reduce to a very low heat and simmer for 2 minutes.
7. Transfer to a bowl then add the breadcrumbs, pecan nuts and flax seeds and mix through. Cover with a tea towel and leave to cool.

Wellington Method:

1. Place the readymade pastry on a floured surface.
2. Layer some Aubergine & Mushroom Pesto in the middle of the pastry, being careful to avoid the edges. (Leave a 2cm gap away from the edge to allow for folding).
3. 3Place your cooled filling mixture on top of the aubergine pesto.
4. Baste the edges of the pastry with warm water using a pastry brush.
5. Begin to fold and form the wellington making sure all edges are sealed and tucked in securely.
6. Place the wellington on parchment paper then on a baking tray and cook in the oven at 200oC/gas mark 7/8 for 20/25 mins or until golden brown.

Tip: You can glaze the top with molasses or golden syrup for a lovely shiny glaze before roasting.

Aubergine & Mushroom Jackfruit Pizza

Jackfruit is grown in many tropical countries including the Caribbean and we've teamed it with our pesto for this quick and easy pizza treat.

Serves 4

100g Jackfruit (fresh or tinned)
1 Pizza base readymade.
½ Orange pepper, sliced.
½ Yellow pepper, sliced.
50g Vegan

Cheese, grated.
2 Spring Onions, sliced.
1 jar Aubergine & Mushroom Pesto & Spread.
1 tbsp Fresh thyme (optional)
1 tbsp Fresh

Basil (optional)

Method:

1. Spread a layer of the pesto evenly onto a pizza base.
2. Arrange the jackfruit, herbs and peppers on top of the aubergine pesto.
3. Sprinkle the vegan cheese over the top.
4. Place in a pre-heated oven 220oC/gas mark 8 for 15/18 minutes and serve.

Tip:

It's best to use fresh jackfruit you can buy from Chinese supermarkets. If not, you can use the tinned varieties from general supermarkets, Asian stores or you can buy it online.

Jerk Mushroom Burger

Jazz up a mushroom burger with this recipe. It's super easy, very tasty and perfect for summer lunches with some fries and a rum punch!

Serves 4

500g White mushrooms, diced.
150g Bread-crumbs
1 White onion finely chopped.
2 Garlic cloves finely chopped.
2 tbsp Jerk paste (Dips & Things chapter) or Tan Rosie Jerk Rub.
1 Red chilli finely chopped.
1 tsp Salt
1 tsp Black Pepper
Olive oil
2 tbsp Flax seed in water to form paste.
4 Burger buns
Lettuce leaves
2 Tomatoes

Method:

1. Place a saucepan on a medium heat, add 3 tbsp olive oil and fry the white onion for 2 minutes until softened.
2. Add the chopped mushroom and cook for 3 minutes.
3. Add the garlic, salt, black pepper, chilli and jerk paste/rub then cook for a further 2 minutes.
4. 4Remove from heat, then add the breadcrumbs, flax seeds and mix through.
5. Transfer to a bowl, cover with tea towel and leave to cool down.
6. Once the mushroom mixture has completely cooled, form into 4 patties and place on parchment paper on a baking tray.
7. Cook in the oven at 200oC/gas mark 7 for 40 minutes.
8. Remove from oven and leave to rest for 5 minutes before forming your burger.
9. To form the burger layer slices of lettuce, tomato, red onion and your choice of sauce with your mushroom burger and serve with fries. Enjoy!

Tip:

We used our Banana Ketchup on the burger pictured which added extra Caribbean flavour to the burger.

Chickpea & Sweet Potato Balls in a Coconut Garlic Sauce

This is recipe is a great way to use readily available Caribbean ingredients in a new way. We've used or plantain crisps as a gluten free crumb to coat these tasty balls and added extra Caribbean flavour with this very garlicky coconut sauce.

Makes 14 balls

Sauce Ingredients:

5 Garlic cloves finely chopped.
1 tbsp Fresh thyme finely chopped.
1 Tin coconut milk
250ml Vegan coconut cream
1 White onion
finely chopped.
Olive Oil
1 tsp Salt
1 tsp Black Pepper
1 tbsp Cornflour

Balls Ingredients:

2 tins Chickpeas, drained.
500g Sweet potato, peeled & diced
1 White onion finely diced.
2 Garlic cloves finely chopped.
1 tbsp fresh thyme finely chopped.
½ tsp Salt
½ tsp Black Pepper
1 tbsp Flax seeds in water to form paste.
1 tsp Vegetable stock
1 pack Tan Rosie Plantain Crisps

Balls Filling Method:

1. Boil the sweet potato in lightly salted water in a saucepan until cooked, drain and put to one side.
2. Place a saucepan on a medium heat, add 3 tbsp olive and fry the onions for 3 minutes until softened.
3. Add the chickpeas and cook for 1 minute.
4. Add the sweet potato, garlic, thyme, salt, black pepper, stock and stir. Cook for a further 3 minutes on a low heat.
5. Remove from heat, transfer to a bowl, cover with a tea towel and leave to rest until completely cool.

Sauce Method:

1. Place a saucepan on a medium heat, add the chopped onion and cook until softened for 3 minutes. Add the garlic, thyme, salt, black pepper and stir.
2. Add the coconut milk, cornflour, coconut cream, stir and bring to the boil and thicken.
3. Adjust thickness with extra cornflour if needed, then transfer to a food blender and process into a smooth sauce.
4. Leave to one side.

Balls Method:

1. Crush the plantain crisps into fine crumbs in a food processor and place on a plate.
2. Using a dessert spoon, spoon some of mixture into your hand to form a ball. Roll it in the plantain crumb making sure it's coated evenly and then place on parchment paper on a baking tray. Repeat the process until all the mixture is used. Cook in the oven at 200oC/gas mark 7 for 25 minutes.
3. Serve the balls on a bed of white rice with the coconut garlic sauce poured over the top. Delicious!

Tofu Pelau

Pelau is a traditional dish cooked in Grenada and many other Caribbean islands. It takes inspiration from Indian cuisine and is essentially a one-pot dish combining peas, beans, rice with chicken. We've used tofu as a perfect meat replacement for this dish.

Serves 4

2 cups/500g Long grain rice washed	*Stock*	*Thyme*
1 tin Kidney beans drained.	*1 Medium white onion finely chopped.*	*2 tbsp Tan Rosie's Jerk Rub*
280g Firm Tofu, diced	*2 Garlic cloves finely chopped.*	*1 Small red chilli/scotch bonnet finely chopped*
1 tin Coconut Milk	*3 tsp Salt*	*Olive Oil*
400ml Vegetable	*1 tsp Black Pepper*	
	1 tbsp Fresh	

Method:

1. Place the diced tofu in a bowl. Drizzle with olive and rub in the jerk seasoning until coated.
2. Fry the tofu in a pan until golden brown and set to one side.
3. Place a saucepan on a medium heat then add 3 tbsp olive oil then add the onions and fry for 3 minutes until softened.
4. Add the garlic, thyme, salt, black pepper, kidney beans, chilli and stir.
5. Add the rice and stir.
6. Add the coconut milk, vegetable stock, stir and bring to the boil.
7. Reduce the heat to a very low setting, cover and cook for 15 minutes.
8. After 15 minutes, and the tofu, stir and replace the cover and cook for a further 10 minutes or until the rice is cooked.
9. Check the rice to see if it's cooked, if so, remove from the heat replace the lid and leave to absorb any extra liquid for 5 minutes then serve.

Sweet Potato & Red Lentil Cottage Pie

Lorem ipsum dolor sit amet, consectetuer adipiscing elit, sed diam nonummy nibh euismod tincidunt ut laoreet dolore magna aliquam erat volutpat. Ut wisi enim ad minim veniam, quis nostrud exerci tation ullamcorper suscipit lobortis nisl ut aliquip ex ea commodo consequat.

Serves 4

2 cups/500g Long grain rice washed
1 tin Kidney beans drained.
280g Firm Tofu, diced
1 tin Coconut Milk
400ml Vegetable Stock

1 Medium white onion finely chopped.
2 Garlic cloves finely chopped.
3 tsp Salt
1 tsp Black Pepper
1 tbsp Fresh Thyme

2 tbsp Tan Rosie's Jerk Rub
1 Small red chilli/scotch bonnet finely chopped
Olive Oil

Method:

1. Place the diced tofu in a bowl. Drizzle with olive and rub in the jerk seasoning until coated.
2. Fry the tofu in a pan until golden brown and set to one side.
3. Place a saucepan on a medium heat then add 3 tbsp olive oil then add the onions and fry for 3 minutes until softened.
4. Add the garlic, thyme, salt, black pepper, kidney beans, chilli and stir.
5. Add the rice and stir.
6. Add the coconut milk, vegetable stock, stir and bring to the boil.
7. Reduce the heat to a very low setting, cover and cook for 15 minutes.
8. After 15 minutes, and the tofu, stir and replace the cover and cook for a further 10 minutes or until the rice is cooked.
9. Check the rice to see if it's cooked, if so, remove from the heat replace the lid and leave to absorb any extra liquid for 5 minutes then serve.

Red Pepper Stew with Pumpkin Dumplings

We eat many different types of stews in the Caribbean, and you can pretty much add any ingredient you prefer. We've teamed red peppers with kidney beans and added in some tasty pumpkin dumplings. It's a hearty stew and extremely yummy!

Serves 4

Stew Ingredients:

Dumping Ingredients:

4 Large Red Bell Peppers 1 inch diced
1 Tin Kidney beans, drained
1 Large red onion finely diced
2 Tins Chopped Tomatoes
3 Garlic cloves diced
300ml Vegetable

3 Carrots diced
2 Celery sticks diced
Olive Oil
1 tbsp Fresh Thyme
2 tbsp Smoked Paprika
1 Small Red chilli finely chopped
2 tbsp Tan Rosie Garlic &

Pepper Hot Sauce flavour) finely crushed in food processor.

1 cup/250g Self Raising Flour
½ tsp Salt
1 tsp Sugar
Nut Milk to combine.
2 tbsp Olive Oil
100g Pumpkin, peeled diced, boiled and pureed.

Dumpling Method:

1. In a mixing bowl, add the self-raising flour, olive oil and salt, sugar, then mix into crumbs.
2. Add the pureed pumpkin and knead (add extra flour if it becomes too sticky).
3. Add the nut milk a little at a time to the flour to create a soft dough.
4. Cover with a tea towel or cling film and rest for 20 mins.
5. Once rested, on a floured surface, knead for 1 minute then form small round and flat dumplings (makes around 12).

Stew Method:

1. Place a large saucepan on a medium heat and add 3 tbsp olive, add the onions and cook for 1 minutes until softened.
2. Add the carrots and celery and cook for 3 minutes stirring.
3. Add the garlic, salt, black pepper, thyme, chilli, red peppers, smoked paprika and stir.
4. Add the tomatoes, hot sauce, vegetable stock and kidney beans and stir. Bring to the boil.
5. Add the dumplings to the saucepan being careful not to damage them and lightly stir. Cover, lower heat, and simmer for 20 minutes or until the dumplings are firm and cooked.
6. Check the seasoning and serve.

Polenta Pumpkin Pie

Polenta is also known as 'Coo Coo' in many parts of the Caribbean and it can be combined with a variety of ingredients to make savoury dishes. Have a go at this quick and easy pie great for supper or lunch.

Serves 3/4

250g Pumpkin peeled, diced.
1 Red bell pepper, diced.
250g/1 cup Polenta
1 Medium White Onion
2 Garlic cloves
1 Small

Red/green Chilli diced.
300ml Vegetable Stock
100g Vegan Cheese, grated.
1 tin/250ml Coconut milk
½ tsp Salt
½ tsp Black

Pepper
1 tbsp Fresh Rosemary
1 tbsp Fresh Thyme
Olive Oil

Method:

1. Place a saucepan on a medium heat and 3 tbsp olive oil. Add the onions and fry for 3 minutes until softened.
2. Add the garlic, chilli, salt, black pepper, and bell pepper and stir.
3. Add the vegetable stock, thyme, rosemary, coconut milk, cheese and stir.
4. Once boiled, at the polenta and with a whisk continuously whisk for 2/3 minutes until everything is combined to cook through.
5. Remove from the heat and place in a greased dish and leave to cool to firm up.
6. Once cooled, slice into wedges (reheat if required) and serve with a salad or steamed veg. Enjoy!

Tip:

This dish can be eaten hot or cold.

Green Banana Gnocchi

Try this twist on Italian gnocchi using green bananas! You can also use green plantain too. Stir in your favourite pesto or try our Aubergine & Mushroom Pesto & Spread..

Serves 3/4

3 Green Bananas
(or 2 green
plantain)
peeled & sliced
1cm
½ cup Plain
Flour
Nut milk

Method:

1. In a pan boil the chopped green banana for 5 minutes until cooked.
2. Drain and place in a food processor with a few tablespoons of nut milk to loosen, then blend until smooth.
3. On a floured surface, place the green banana and the flour, then knead until all the flour has been incorporated into the green banana to form a dough.
4. Cut the dough into 3 or pieces and then roll into long 'snakes' about 1cm thick.
5. Cut into 1 inch pieces and repeat until all dough has been used.
6. Place the gnocchi in a pan of boiling water to cook for 3 minutes. Do not crowd the pan with too much gnocchi, split into 2 batches.
7. Once each batch is cooked, place in a bowl and mix with your favourite pesto or pasta sauce and serve.

Tip:

1. This dish can be eaten hot or cold.
2. The gnocchi can be fried off in olive oil to add extra colour and flavour.

Pigeon Pea Pumpkin Wraps

Pigeon peas make a delicious wrap filling for sandwiches. We've teamed this with the pumpkin flatbread recipe in the 'bakes' section of this book and refer to the 'dips & things' section for the pigeon pea mash filling. Add some vegan mayo, salad, and hot sauce for extra yumminess!

Serves 2

2 Pumpkin Wrap
(see 'Bakes'
section for
recipe)
Pigeon Pea &
Garlic Spread
(see 'Dips &
Things' section
for recipe)
Lettuce leaves

1 Tomato
Red Onion
Vegan Mayo
Tan Rosie's
Garlic & Pepper
Sauce HOT
Salt
Black Pepper

Method:

1. Lay the flat bread on a chopping board, then layer the pigeon pea spread.
2. Add some mayo and hot sauce.
3. Layer salad, and sauces to create your wrap. Easy!

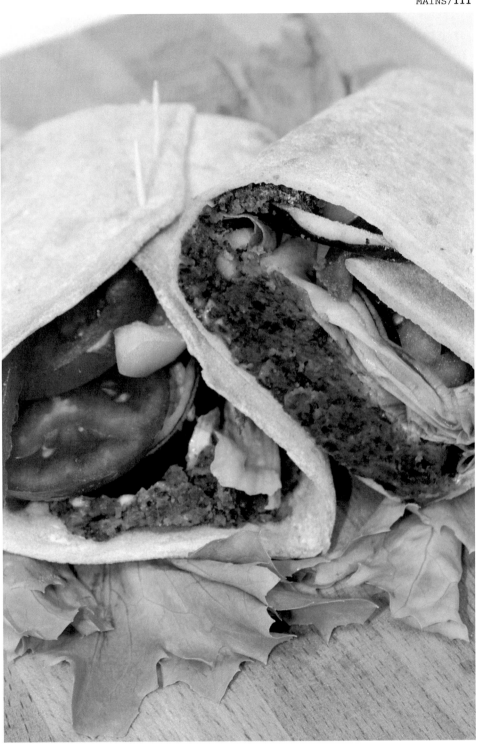

Desserts

Crunchy Ginger Chocolate Biscuits

Ginger is a popular spice ingredient we've used within our family for generations, and we love to use it in both savoury and sweet dishes. Cocoa beans grow all over Grenada making delicious chocolate, and we couldn't help spreading over these biscuits!

Makes 12/14

200g Vegan Margarine/butter
100g Brown Sugar
300g Plain Flour
200g Glace Ginger roughly chopped

1 tsp Ginger extract
150g Dark Vegan Chocolate
½ tsp Salt

Method:

1. In a mixing bowl, place the butter and sugar and combine until smooth.
2. Then add the flour, glace ginger, ginger extract, salt and form into a dough.
3. Place back into bowl, cover with cling film and place in the fridge to cool for 1 hour.
4. Once cooled, roll out onto a floured surface, and use a pastry cutter, cut into round biscuits.
5. Once you have cut all the biscuits, place on parchment paper on a baking tray and cook at 175oC/189oC/gas mark 4/5 for 10/12 minutes until golden brown.
6. Once cooked, place on a cooling rack until cool.
7. Melt the dark chocolate in a bain-marie (take a pan of boiling water, place another glass or metal bowl in the water, then add the chocolate to melt).
8. Dip your biscuits in the chocolate then place on a cooling rack and eat!

Coconut Rum & Raisin Ice Cream

This is probably one of the best ice cream recipes Monica has created and it's totally vegan! It's super creamy, indulgent and it will leave you wanting more!

Serves 6

1 tin Coconut Custard
1 tin Condensed coconut milk
250ml Vegan whipped Cream
1 Tin Coconut evaporated milk
1 tsp Vanilla Extract

1 tsp Angostura Bitters (optional)
½ tsp sea salt
½ cup Maple Syrup
1 Cup Rum and Raisins
½ tsp Ground nutmeg

½ tsp Ground Cinnamon

Equipment:
Ice cream maker
or
Handheld whisk
Large bowl

Equipment:
Ice cream maker
or
Handheld whisk
Large bowl

Method:

1. Combine all ingredients and whisk in large mixing bowl.
2. Whisk together until combined.
3. Transfer to an ice cream maker and churn / mix until fluffy approximately 40 minutes.
4. Transfer to a freezer container and store in freezer.
5. Alternatively, after whipping transfer to a freezer container and freeze for about 2 hours, then whip again and return to freezer to set.

Cassava Pone

Cassava Pone is a traditional Caribbean dessert using freshly grated cassava. You can also add grated coconut to the mixture to add extra Caribbean flavour

Serves 6

4 cups Cassava peeled & grated finely.
1 ½ cups Brown sugar
6 tbsp Vegan margarine/butter
1 tsp Cinnamon
½ tsp Nutmeg

1 tsp Almond Extract
1 tin/32og Vegan Condensed Milk
1 Cup Nut milk

Method:

1. Preheat the oven to 180oC.
2. In a large mixing bowl place all ingredients and mix thoroughly until smooth.
3. Pour the mixture inti a greased oven/cake tin and cook in the oven for 1 hour until the cassava is melted and smooth.
4. Once cooked, remove from the oven and leave to rest to set and cool. Slice into cubed and serve with cream, ice cream or yoghurt.

Tip:

1. When you are preparing the cassava, make sure you remove and discard the stringy, fibrous section in the middle of the cassava, as this does not break down when cooking.
2. Some specialist Asian stores have frozen grated cassava.

Polenta Banana Pudding

Sweetened polenta tastes great in a dessert especially with banana. It can be eaten hot or cold with this yummy, sticky rum sauce and maybe a dollop of ice cream!

Serves 4

Polenta Ingredients:

250g Polenta
3 Bananas
mashed/blended.
2 Bananas
sliced.
400ml Coconut
Milk
1 tsp Cinnamon
1 tsp Vanilla
Extract

125g Light
Brown Sugar
¼ tsp Salt

Rum Sauce Ingredients:

¼ Cup Dark Rum
½ Cup Brown
Sugar
1 tsp Molasses
2 tbsp Vegan
Butter

Sauce Method:

1. Place all the sauce ingredients into a small saucepan and bring to boil to thicken.
2. Once it's thickened sufficiently, remove from the heat and cover.

Sliced Banana Method:

1. Slice 1 banana 0.5cm width pieces.
2. Add 2 tbsp brown sugar in a non-stick frying pan on a medium heat. Once the sugar turns light brown add the banana slices and caramelise and fry for 1 to 2 minutes.

Polenta Method:

1. Place a saucepan on a medium heat, add the coconut milk, cinnamon, vanilla extract, salt, mashed bananas and stir.
2. Bring to the boil and add the polenta and stir continuously with a whisk for 2 minutes.
3. Line a dish roughly 4/5 inch in height with parchment paper, then pour half of rum sauce.
4. Layer the slices of caramalised banana over the rum sauce ensuring that the pieces do not layer over each other.
5. Pour over the polenta and smooth out.
6. Leave to cool in the fridge for a few hours or until fully set (it can be left overnight if desired).
7. Once it has fully set, turn out onto a serving plate and slice into sections. Pour over the remaining rum sauce over each piece and serve with ice cream or yoghurt.

Glossary

Weights & Measurements

Gas Mark	Fahrenheit	Celsius	Description
1/4	225	110	Very cool/very slow
1/2	250	130	---
1	275	140	cool
2	300	150	---
3	325	170	---
4	350	180	---
5	375	190	---
6	400	200	moderate
7	425	220	hot
8	450	230	---
9	475	240	very hot

1 tablespoon (tbsp) =	3 teaspoons (tsp)
1/16 cup =	1 tablespoon
1/8 cup =	2 tablespoons
1/6 cup =	2 tablespoons + 2 teaspoons
1/4 cup =	4 tablespoons
1/3 cup =	5 tablespoons + 1 teaspoon
3/8 cup =	6 tablespoons
1/2 cup =	8 tablespoons
2/3 cup =	10 tablespoons + 2 teaspoons
3/4 cup =	12 tablespoons
1 cup =	230g
8 fluid ounces (fl oz) =	1 cup
1 pint (pt) =	2 cups
1 quart (qt) =	2 pints
4 cups =	1 quart
1 gallon (gal) =	4 quarts
16 ounces (oz) =	1 pound (lb)
1 milliliter (ml) =	1 cubic centimeter (cc)
1 inch (in) =	2.54 centimeters (cm)

Capacity		Weight	
1/5 teaspoon	1 milliliter	1 oz	28 grams
1 teaspoon	5 ml	1 pound	454 grams
1 tablespoon	15 ml		
1 fluid oz	30 ml		
1/5 cup	47 ml		
1 cup	237 ml		
2 cups (1 pint)	473 ml		
4 cups (1 quart)	.95 liter		
4 quarts (1 gal.)	3.8 liters		

Index

Index

A
Allsipe/Pimento 20
Aubergine
    Veggie Info:Other Fruit & Vegetables 18
    Aubergine & Mushroom Jackfruit Pizza 94
    Green Bananan Gnocchi 108

B
Bakes 25
    Pumpkin Flatbread 26
    Callaloo Roti 28
    Plantain Bread 30
    ASweet Potato & Thyme Rolls 32
    Plantain Stuffed Fried Dumplings 34
Banana
    Veggie Info: Plantain & Green Banana 16
    Green Banana Gnocchi 108
    Polenta Banana Pudding 120
    Banana Ketchup 8
Beans
    Veggie Info: Pulses & Grains 10
    Black Bean & Coconut Stew 48
    Red Pepper Stew with Pumpkin Dumplings 104

C
Cassava
    Veggie Info: Roots 14
    Hard Food Salad 74
    Cassava Pone 118
Cashew Nuts
    Curried Sweet Potato & Cashew Nut Soup 52
    Baked Curry Cauliflower 82
Cinnamon
    Veggie Info: Spices 20
    Crunchy Ginger Chocolate Biscuits 114
    Coconut Rum & Raisin Ice Cream 116
    Cassava Pone 118
    Polenta Banana Pudding 120
Clove
    Veggie Info: Spices 20
Cauliflower
    Baked Curry Caulifower 82
Corn
    Veggie Info: Other Fruit & Vegetables 18
    Spicy Rice Corn Fritters 38
    Roastesd Corn & Red Pepper Dip 62
    Bajan Style Cou Cou & Okra 78
    Polenta Pumpkin Pie 106
    Polenta Banana Pudding 120
Callaloo

Veggie Info: Greens 12
Callaloo Roti 28
Coconut
    Veggie Info: Other Fruit & Vegetables 18
    Curry Rice & Peas 42
    Black Bean & Coconut Stew 48
    Curried Sweet Potato & Cashew Nut Soup 52
    Roastes Pumpkin & Coconut Spread 64
    Black Eye Pea & Sweet Potato Curry 88
    Chickpea & Sweet Potato Balls in Garlic Coconut Sauce 98
    Tofu Pelau 100
    Polenta Pumpkin Pie 106
    Coconut Rum & Raisin Ice Cream 116
    Polenta Banana Pudding 120
Curry
    Curry Rice & Peas 42
    Curried Sweet Potato & Cashew Nut Soup 52
    Black Eye Pea & Sweet Potato Curry 88
    Tan Rosie Caribbean Style Curry Powder 8
Christophene
    Veggie Info: Greens 12

D
Dumplings
    Plantain Stuffed Fried Dumplings 34
    Pigeon Pea & Corn Dumpling Soup 50
Desserts 113
Dips 57

E
Eddoe/Coco
    Veggie Info: Roots 14
    Hard Food Salad 74

F
Fritters
    Spicy Rice Corn Fritters 38
    Curry Chickpea Fritters 72
Flatbread
    Pumpkin Flatbread 26

G
Ginger
    Veggie Info: Spices 20
    Jerk Paste 58
    Crunchy Ginger Chocolate Biscuits 114
Garlic
    Veggie Info: Traditional Seasoning Combos 22
    Pigeon Pea & Garlic Spread 66

H
Hard Food Salad 74

J

Jackfruit
    Veggie Info: Other Fruit & Vegetables 18
    Aubergine & Mushroom Jackfruit Pizza 94
Jerk
    Tan Rosie's Jerk Rub 8
    Jerk Paste 58
    Jerk Roastes Pumpkin 70
    Jerk Tofu Skewers 90
    Jerk Mushroom Burger 96
    Tofu Pelau 100

L

Lentils
    Green Lentil & Plantain Stew 54
    Vehhie Info: Pulses & Grains 10
    Caribbean Wellington 92
    Sweet Potato & Red Lentil Cottage Pie 102
Lime
    Veggie Info: Other Fruit & Vegetables 18
    Okra Fried Rice 44
    Lime Chilli Whole Baked Plantain 80

M

Mains 85

O

Onion
    Veggie Info: Traditional Seasoning Combos 22
Okra
    Veggie Info: Greens 12
    Bajan Style Cou Cou & Okra 78
    Okra Fried Rice 44

P

Plantain
    Veggie Info: Plantain & Green Banana 16
    Tan Rosie Plantain Crisps 8
    Plantain Bread 30
    Plantain Stuffed Fried Dumplings 34
    Lime Chilli Whole Baked Plantain 80
    Green Plantain Rosti 76
Pumpkin
    Veggie Info: Other Fruit & Vegetables 18
    Pumpkin Flatbread 26
    Roastes Pumpkin & Coconut Spread 64
    Jerk Roasted Pumpkin 70
    Pumpkin Macaroni Pie 86
Pepper
    Veggie Info: Spices 18, 20, 22
    Tan Rosie Garlic & Pepper Sauce HOT 8
Polenta: See Corn section

Red Pepper Spiced Rice 40
Jerk Paste 58
Lime Chilli Whole Baked Plantain 80
Red Pepper Stew with Pumpkin Dumplings 104
Polenta Pumpkin Pie 106
Okra Fried Rice 44

Peas
    Veggie Info: Pulses & Grains 10
    Curry Rice & Peas 42
    Pigeon Pea & Corn Dumpling Soup 50
    Pigeon Pea & Garlic SPread 66
    Black Eye Pea Dip 60
    Curry Chickpea Fritters 72
    Black Eye Pea & Sweet Potato Curry 88
    Chickpea & Sweet Potato Balls in Garlic Coconut Sauce 98
    Pigeon pea Pumpkin Wrap 110

Potato
Sweet Potato, Red
    Veggie Info: Roots 14
    Sweet Potato & Thyme Rolls 32
    Chickpea & Sweet Potato Balls in Garlic Coconut Sauce 98
    Sweet Potato & Red Lentil Cottage Pie 102

Sweet Potato, White
    Veggie InfoL Roots 14

R

Rice
    Veggie Info: Pulses & Grains 10
    Spicy Rice Corn Fritters 38
    Red Pepper Spiced Rice 40
    Curry Rice & PEas 42
    Okra Fried Rice 44
    Tofu Pelau 100

Rum
    Coconut Rum & Raisin Ice Cream 116
    Polenta Banana Pudding 120

Roti
    Callaloo Roti 28

S

Soup
    Pigeon Pea & Corn Dumpling Soup 50
    Curries Sweet Potaot Cashew Nut Soup 52

Salad
    Hard Food Salald 74

Stews
    Balck Bean & Coconut Stew 48
    Green Lentil & Plantain Stew 54

Y

Yam
    Veggie Info: Roots 14
    Hard Food Sald 74